DEPRESSION

A Christian Woman's Journey

By Julie K Miles

CONTENTS

Introduction..4

What is depression? 5

Depression is awful – But there is Hope! – Depression is different for everyone

Causes of depression 9

How I experience depression

Some possible related symptoms 14

Burning brain – Brain fog

Helpful things to know 16

Worst fears – Feeling worse in the mornings – shame

You are not your thoughts 18

Intrusive thoughts – Core beliefs

The journey through 23

What you need and what will help on the journey 27

Changing our thoughts 29

Faith and meaning ……………………………………..33

Encouragement from the Bible - Not just in our own strength

Spiritual input …………………………………………35

Thankfulness –Prayer – Hope – A testimony

Getting out of the vicious circle …………………..48

Things will get better

The good that comes from depression………..51

Seasons

What helps? ……………………………………………..53

Anti-depressants – Cognitive Behavioural Therapy – Creativity – Meditation - Exercise

Famous people who have struggled with depression ………………………………………………..58

Conclusion……………………………………………….59

Books I've found helpful ……………………………61

About the author ……………………………………..62

Introduction

I hope you will find this book helpful. I am writing it in the belief that I have gained some insight over the years in dealing with periods of depression, and I am hopeful that this insight may help you on your journey.

I know there are plenty of books out there on the subject of getting through depression, and I have read a few of them(!), but perhaps I can put things in a different way that will help you. I will endeavour to make it easy to read and refer to.

I have to admit that I have started to write it partly for my own benefit too, in order to get my thoughts out as I have been and am currently, as I write, working through depression myself. As a fellow sufferer I hope you will know that you are not alone and that some of my thoughts will resonate with you and validate your experience too.

I think I should let you know that I write from the standpoint and worldview of being a believer in Jesus and trying to follow him. That inevitably affects my writing and journey through depression but please don't let it put you off if you do not have that experience. There will still be help here.

What is depression?

My Pocket Oxford Dictionary (1984 edition) defines depression as a "State of extreme dejection often with physical symptoms".

The NHS website helpfully says:

"Some people think depression is trivial and not a genuine health condition. They're wrong – it is a real illness with real symptoms. Depression is not a sign of weakness or something you can 'snap out of' by 'pulling yourself together'."

It goes on to say that most people with help, go on to make a full recovery.

That is good news for us. Thankfully there is more understanding and help available these days, but there still remains some stigma I believe. It is difficult for people who have never experienced depression to really understand what it is like to do so.

Depression is about feeling very down and hopeless, finding little if any enjoyment in life, but also often with accompanying physical symptoms – low energy; wanting to sleep more or being unable to sleep; eating more or not wanting to eat. It is often accompanied with anxiety and unusual or negative disturbing thoughts.

Personally, I find the mental and emotional side of things to be the most prominent aspect of depression. However, our whole bodies are interconnected. Our physical, mental and emotional selves all affect each other. None of them are separate. For example, if we are physically ill, we often feel down too. This can be good news too as if we influence one part positively, it affects the other parts in a good way. For example, if you go for a walk, it affects us mentally and emotionally, lifting our mood. Making ourselves a cup of tea and a snack also lifts our mood. The physical is impacting the mental and emotional. It works the other way too. If we think positive thoughts such as being grateful for something, it can make us feel better emotionally. However, you cannot just think yourself out of depression by thinking positive thoughts. It's not quite that simple in my experience at least. So, we see that depression is an illness that affects us mentally, physically and emotionally.

Depression is awful

Someone has said that depression is the worst pain known to man. I don't know if that is true or not, but when you're in it, it certainly feels like it! It truly is awful. The pits.

But there is Hope!

There is always hope. Light at the end of the tunnel. Always hang on to that!

Depression is different for everyone

Another point worth noting is that everyone's experience of depression is unique.

I am having some CBT (Cognitive Behavioural Therapy) counselling at the moment and one of the first questions my counsellor asked me was "How do you experience depression?". This made me realise that he knew that everyone experiences it differently.

There are common symptoms, which you realise when you are asked to do one of the questionnaires used by a health professional to assess the severity of your depression. They ask you to score your symptoms from "not at all" to "every day". These relate to your levels of energy, tiredness, how well you are sleeping, your eating, ability to do everyday tasks, enjoyment of life, ability to feel you can socialise etc. However, your depression will be unique to you because you are a unique individual.

Personally, I experience depression as feeling very low in mood and starting to have unpleasant and very negative thoughts. Sometimes I have felt like I'm going mad and am out of control. It's a very frightening feeling. Because our experience is unique, it can make us feel very isolated. But you are not alone. There is help. I want to emphasise to you that you can and will get better. Even when you feel that is not the case. Depression causes us to think the worst-case scenario is true. It isn't.

Causes of depression

The causes of depression will vary from one person to another.

Often depression is connected to loss of some kind. Maybe it's due to a bereavement; maybe a loss of health; maybe a loss of control; or a job loss or retirement or simply getting older – a loss of our youth. There are numerous losses we can and do experience in life.

Sometimes depression comes in reaction to a traumatic event or abuse of some sort. The abuse may have been recent or in the past. Sometimes depression can come on quickly but often there is some kind of build up to it. You sometimes hear people say "things have got on top of me". Too many of those "things" on top of us can really bring us down.

In my latest period of depression, there has been a long build up to it. Personally, I had a difficult marriage and had to leave the marital home over 7 years ago now. Since then, I have gone through divorce, both my parents have died and I have moved twice including into my own home. I've also had 3 different jobs and am now retired. All of that has been a lot of change and loss in the space of those years.

When there is change like that, we can lose sight of who we are – a kind of loss of identity. Who am I now? I'm no longer a wife or a daughter, I'm a single, divorced woman. Whilst those labels are factually true, that isn't who I really am. And who I really am is what I need to find out. I need to "return to myself". Perhaps depression involves a death of a part of us in order that a new self can emerge. I think that throughout life we have to "re-invent" ourselves to one degree or another according to the stage of life we find ourselves in.

A vicar once said to me that he thought that God was sometimes working behind the scenes or "doing something behind the depression" when people get depressed. That kind of helped at the time.

I have heard psychologists say that we can go into depressions to mask trauma or cover up what is painful to us. Kind of like "I can't look at that right now so I'll shut down and get depressed." Of course, this is not a conscious decision. The human body and psyche are amazing. Personally, I think I would rather face up to things than be depressed but perhaps my mind and body know better.

Depression can also be the result of messages received in childhood or where depression is in the family. This is partly the case in my family as I believe both my parents struggled with depression at points in their lives. My mum, as a child in London, lived through "the Depression" but I don't know if that counts, but certainly she and her family moved around a lot from rented basements to other rented accommodation and her father was out of work a lot of the time. It wasn't an easy childhood, which obviously affected her.

How I experience depression

As I've said previously, everyone's experience of depression is unique because everyone is a unique individual. How I experience depression will be different to you, but there may be some similarities and that may help you see you are not on your own.

In this current period of depression, I started feeling hopeless and thinking negative thoughts like "What's the purpose of my life now?" and "I'm getting old and who will be there for me?"

As I am in my mid-60's and divorced and retired from paid work, this obviously relates to the stage of life I'm in now and are really logical and valid questions to ask, but the feeling behind them was that I was struggling to feel I had a purpose and felt very much on my own and isolated. I also started feeling strange sensations in my head and began to feel desperate. At one stage I felt a burning sensation in my brain and a google search told me that there was, indeed, such a thing and that this can be related to depression. I will come back to this later.

As I said, the thoughts I was having were valid, but in depression, our negative thoughts are magnified and get out of proportion.

It was then that I contacted my GP surgery and was prescribed anti-depressants. To be fair, the GP asked me what I wanted – to be referred for talking therapies or to be prescribed anti-depressants and I chose both. She also asked which anti-depressant I would prefer to take as I had previously been prescribed 3 different ones, all SSRI's. I decided to go back to the one I had first taken 17 years ago and had been on for about a year at that time.

Anti-depressants aren't something I like to take, but I believe they can be a lifeline. A bit like a life belt until we can be rescued. A buffer against the overwhelming sad, unhappy and frightening feelings. One of the reasons I don't like taking anti-depressants is because of the side effects. And yes, all medications have them, so you have to take that into consideration. Having said that, the side effects can diminish over time. However, sometimes it's difficult to know whether what I am experiencing in my head – the woolliness and unpleasant sensations – are the depression or the side-effects. It can be confusing and disturbing.

When I feel these sensations, I feel I need reassurance – is this normal? Do other people experience this too? I have asked both medical professionals and other sufferers, but they don't seem to know what I mean. As I've said, your and my experience is unique. It would be good to have reassurance and that is partly why I'm wanting to share my experiences as they may be a help to other sufferers.

I think we have to navigate our own journey and I hope some of my experience is helpful to you.

Some possible related symptoms

Burning brain

This sensation of your brain feeling like it is burning, is a medical condition, according to a Google search. It can be an indication of something as serious as encephalitis which is inflammation of the brain, but also it can be a symptom relating to depression. No one has ever mentioned this to me and when I asked the GP I saw in relation to this, he had not heard of it, nor had my counsellor.

Our bodies can become inflamed when they are fighting infection, and indeed, it is considered by some health practitioners that inflammation is a major cause of certain illnesses. So, I suppose it stands to reason that the brain can become inflamed when it is not functioning in a healthy manner, such as happens in depression. Thankfully our brains can recover from this and I am no longer having these sensations. Possibly the medication is helping. Certainly, I am feeling more positive now I have been taking it for a couple of months. In addition, it is fair to say that all the things that help our physical health, such as eating healthily (plenty of fruit and veg) and exercise, will help our brain health too.

Brain Fog

I think this is fairly self-explanatory but it means a feeling of fuzziness in your mind and possibly sluggish thinking. It can be related to depression and anxiety. I have struggled with this and as with burning brain, these symptoms can, in themselves, cause you further anxiety and they are unpleasant and you wonder what is going on in your brain. If you are concerned, do chat it over with your GP as they can be symptoms of other conditions too.

I think the important thing is to not get anxious about it as that is self-defeating. If it is related to your depression or anxiety, it will help to get regular walks outside in the fresh air; eat a healthy diet; drink enough water and not eat too much sugar. All these things apply to maintain good general health anyway. Not always easy to do and don't beat yourself up if you don't manage these things. I know I certainly fall short but I keep trying! Who doesn't want cake and chocolate when you're fed up?!!!

Some helpful things to know

Worst fears

A counsellor from the NHS mental health team I once saw, told me that when we are depressed, our worst fears are magnified. It really helped me at the time to know that, as I'd been fearing something terrible would happen to me. The example he gave was that if you are someone who cares deeply about children and hates the thought of a child being abused, you could start to fear that you were a paedophile. That is an extreme example but illustrates how dark and irrational our fears can be. The thing to realise is that they are not true and have got out of proportion.

Feeling worse in the mornings

This can be a "thing" with depression - you wake up feeling "blah". Then the negative thoughts flood in. A Google search informed me that this may be due to our cortisol levels rising as we awake. I've found that getting up and making a cup of tea is the best solution. Start counteracting the negative thoughts with positive ones, do some stretches as moving your body raises your serotonin levels, serotonin being one of your happy hormones. Go for a walk or plan something nice like a coffee with a friend.

Shame

This is something we can feel in depression. Shame that we are depressed at all. Shame about the thoughts we have. Shame that we can't enjoy things that others are enjoying or just get on with our lives. Shame that we need medication. I think this is one of the worst parts of depression, if there is a worst part.

As a Christian, I think this shame can be magnified as we feel we are not supposed to feel like this. We can think that we are meant to be happy and joyful. Yes, but just because you are a Christian doesn't mean you can't be depressed. It is an illness, as described at the beginning of this book.

"I'm not supposed to feel like this" is the title of a very helpful book I would recommend by Chris Williams, Paul Richards and Ingrid Whitton. Chris and Ingrid work in the field of psychiatry and Paul is a pastor of a church. It is primarily written for a Christian audience, but not exclusively.

You are not your thoughts

Or your trauma or your feelings or the depression. You are separate to them and those are experiences that you are having - not you. It can be very difficult to see that when those thoughts are so convincing.

In addition, you are not responsible for the thoughts that come into your mind. More on that later.

Meditation and mindfulness are tools that illustrate this. In both techniques, we are to be in the present and concentrate on our breathing. In meditation, we may think of a word like "peace" and when other thoughts come into our mind (which they will), we just let them go. We don't focus on them and instead just go back to focussing on our breathing and our word. The fact that we can observe the thought and let it go shows that it isn't us.

At the end of the day, it is our thoughts that can cause us the most distress, and managing them will help us greatly,.

To quote from the wise poem Desiderata:

"But do not distress yourself with dark imaginings. Many fears are born of fatigue and loneliness."

I think this is true. My current depression is partly as a result of living on my own and spending too much time on my own, with my own thoughts.

We are social beings and we need community. We need friends and those we can relate to. We especially need them when we are struggling with depression as things get out of proportion in our minds as described above.

Intrusive thoughts

Everyone gets these in some shape or form. They are unwanted, unsolicited thoughts that come into your mind. They could be frightening in some way, unpleasant or suggestive of you doing something unpleasant for example. For example, if you are walking on a cliff path, a thought may come into your mind to go jump off.

Where these thoughts come from or why we have them is open to speculation but trying to stop them or feeling bad because of them is not helpful. Nor, of course, is acting on them. Recognise they are just thoughts and you are not responsible for them. Just don't dwell on them.

Core Beliefs

Core beliefs are basically what we believe at "core" – what we believe deep down about ourselves, the world and others. They are usually formed in our early years from messages we pick up in childhood.

Psychologists say that these beliefs need to change for real change to occur in our experience. For example, a core belief can be that "I am lovable" or equally that "I am not lovable" or "I am a good person" or "I am a bad person". These beliefs will colour our life experience. Therefore, it is vitally important for us to develop self-awareness and recognise what our core beliefs about ourselves are, or at least have some idea. So how do we do this, as usually we are not aware of them, because they have become so much a part of us.

One way may be to sit with our feelings and ask ourselves where these are coming from.

Alex Howard, a well-known trauma counsellor, often uses the expression "You have to feel it to heal it."

Trace that feeling back – Did you feel that hurt/sadness or rejection as a child? Why do you think you felt that? What were the events/words or messages you were receiving that led you to feel like that?

Writing your thoughts out or journaling would be a good way to do this. Or draw a diagram, whatever helps.

You may need to work with a counsellor or therapist in order to really identify your core beliefs. The purpose of this, is not to do an introspective exercise for its own sake, but to help you identify unhelpful beliefs that are holding you back from enjoying a more fulfilling life. Again, to quote, Alex Howard "If you can see it, you don't have to be it."

A breakthrough moment I experienced many years ago was when someone said to me "You've been told all your life that you are weak". That resonated somehow with me at the time and was a bit of an "Aha" moment. To be fair, I had never been "told" I was weak but I realised that because I had been quite a poorly child, I had been over-protected by my parents which had sent the message to me, subconsciously, that I must be vulnerable, hence weak. It was freeing to have that realisation that I wasn't and didn't have to behave as if I was. I have also come to realise that I am a sensitive person and that that is not a weakness but a strength.

There are possibly multiple core beliefs that we can have. One can easily lead to another. For example, believing I was weak could have led to me feeling I was not important or valuable. You get the picture.

We have to replace those core beliefs with the truth. That we are capable, valuable, beautiful etc. This is true because I believe we are made in the image of God and he is good.

Speaking out positive confessions helps, but we can't brainwash ourselves into believing these things – we have to "have a revelation" of them and realise them on a deeper level.

As a believer in Jesus and God, I "know" those beliefs are true. However, it is one thing to acknowledge things in our head, or give mental assent to them, but quite another to really know deep inside they are true and not be shaken from knowing that by circumstances or our own self-doubt.

My advice would be to listen to God speaking to you in your heart telling you how much he loves you and how precious you are to him.

The journey through

There are metaphors that are helpful for understanding and getting through depression.

One is that it is a journey. A journey out of darkness into light, out of confusion into clarity. A journey into hope.

Another metaphor, which Sue Atkinson uses in her book "Climbing out of Depression" is rock climbing. I think her analogy is very helpful and I would highly recommend her book. She describes being in depression as like finding yourself at the bottom of the rock face, faced with the climb ahead. Sometimes you just have to crawl into a cave there until you are ready to face the climb. That climb, when you start it, may find you starting and then finding yourself back at the bottom again, but at least you are trying to make progress.

For me, the analogy of a journey is helpful as I think life is a journey. There are difficult bits as well as lovely parts. Being in depression could be seen as being stuck in a bog and not knowing how you are going to get out. Probably you will need help. That help can be professional, as in through the GP and medication and/or accessing counselling or "talking therapies" as they are now called. They are available via the

NHS and free or you can find your own therapist privately (from £40 per session) or through a voluntary agency where it is less expensive and you pay according to your means. I have accessed counselling via all three sectors and would recommend any of them. Having someone who is kind and will listen to you is therapeutic in itself. A good therapist can see patterns in your life or thinking that you may not be able to see yourself. They are usually caring, compassionate people who want to help, in my experience.

Being "heard" is something we all need and often don't find it in everyday life. Having friends is important but sometimes they don't always understand you and are not always in the best place themselves to help.

On your journey, you will need to rest. Getting out of a bog takes effort and energy and you will get tired. They say sleep is a great healer. Apparently when you sleep, the synovial fluid in your spinal cord helps detox your brain. If you are struggling to sleep, then rest, listening to soothing music.

Sometimes on a journey, we get lost or we don't know exactly what route we will be taking. That's okay but it can cause anxiety. Don't freak out or panic. It's all okay. It happens. Sometimes we have to rely on our inner satnav to get us to the next stage. Also known as intuition.

Also on a journey, we also experience various kinds of weather. Rain, sleet, snow, even thunderstorms, until the sun comes out again. Often in the North of England, where I live, it is raining or overcast, but the sun eventually breaks through.

Depression can be like a heavy cloud over our minds. For me, music helps to lift the cloud. I enjoy praise and worship music and I also enjoy singing. Sometimes when I sing to God, the darkness and cloud breaks open and the sun shines through.

When we start out on a journey, we have to know where our destination is – where we are aiming for, what we are travelling towards. Yes, of course, we want to feel better and enjoy life again; but what does that look like?

The reason we are depressed may well be that our life is not working for us the way it has been. For me, living on my own, feeling isolated and spiralling down into negative thinking, wondering what my purpose was in life now, led to depression.

Depression has made me realise that I had not been accepting the reality of my life and not facing up to things, but wanting it to have been different, and often putting the blame on others for not meeting my needs. I realise that that is unrealistic. Everyone has their own issues and challenges. I realised I needed to accept my situation in life now and make the best of it I can. I need to be thankful for what I have and recognise what I still have to offer and build on that.

So, my destination and purpose are to use gifts and talents and help others where I can. Also, to do things that I enjoy and that make me happy. My career was in social work in seeking to help people. I can still help people outside of a career.

I think it helps to have a good destination and purpose in mind, no matter what it is and no matter how humble or small it may seem.

What you need and what will help on the journey

Someone said that the journey of 1000 miles starts with one step. So, we just have to start. Sometimes we just have to do something – whatever that might be – rather than wallow in our misery. Go for a walk, ring a friend, ring the GP, wash up or hoover the sitting room floor.

You may need to take medication to help you on your journey – to lift your mood and calm your thoughts. SSRI's stop the serotonin in your brain from being re-absorbed so that you have more of this happy hormone remaining, so you feel better. Well, that's how they think they work. They can take a while to work – even up to 6-8 weeks to get the full benefit. In the meantime, there are likely to be side effects, so you have to persevere. The side effects can be unpleasant and various and you may feel worse before you feel better, so it will take some courage. Getting through depression does take courage but the alternative of staying stuck is not a viable one.

If you do feel bad on the anti-depressants, I would advise ringing your GP again or Mental health service and talk it through with them.

Another help on the journey and one I would recommend is having counselling as I've mentioned before. It helps to have regular appointments so that you know you have that weekly support.

Reassurance is needed on this journey. Let people who you can trust and who care about you know what's going on in your life, so they can support you and maybe check in on you.

If your depression stems from grief, perhaps you can consider grief counselling. Cruse is one service that offers grief counselling and do not charge, but suggest a donation, if you can afford it.

Be patient and kind to yourself. This isn't easy as in my experience, part of depression is that you have a voice in your head that is continually "beating you up" and berating you. We all do have what is known as an "inner critic" according to psychiatrists but when you are depressed, that voice seems to go into overdrive and is harsher and stronger and it's hard to get away from it. It's also sneaky and tries to get you in all different ways. It tells you that your worst fears are true.

Changing our thoughts

When we get depressed, our thoughts are very negative. One of the keys to coming out of depression is recognising those thoughts and changing them. Simple. Yes, but not easy.

The first step is realising that it is possible to change your thinking, but that it is a process that takes persistence. When we are depressed, it is hard to find that resolve and determination to change. That's where I think it helps to know God will help us. It may mean taking anti-depressants too, to lift our mood first.

The next step is recognising those thoughts when we are thinking them. That's not easy as we can become so accustomed to our particular style of thinking that it just feels like that is who we are. However, as I've mentioned before, we are not our thoughts, but they do affect how we are. But we can change them.

The motivation for change is that we obviously want to feel better about ourselves and to be able to enjoy our life. Changing our thoughts from negative to positive plays a big part in this. For example, when I wake up in the morning I often can feel negative thoughts flooding in and rather than dwell on them, which is the path of least resistance, I need to recognise what is happening and stop myself thinking that way and instead say something positive, such as "Thank you God for this new day" or "Thank you God that you love me." Getting up and distracting myself helps too.

I am not suggesting you go around pretending to be happy or putting on a false persona, nor am I talking about denying how you feel and plastering it over with a positive cliché. Rather you are coaching yourself to think differently from the negative patterns you have got into. The danger here is to feel like you're failing and give up. But failing is just part of the process. Get up and try again.

You may need the help of a therapist to help us see the patterns we have in our thinking and identify core beliefs. Having the regular support of another human being does help.

Using positive declarations is a good way to start. You can make up your own or find them online. I would recommend ones that are based on the truth of how God sees us. For example, "God you are my refuge. No matter how bad I feel or how dark my thoughts are, you love me unconditionally."

I know a lady who has surrounded herself with wooden plaques and signs with positive messages on them and has been very intentional about declaring God's words over herself in order to change her thinking. She is a testament to how someone can go from being a negative person with severe mental health problems to a positive person. She still has some mental health challenges but is so much better than she was and is an encouragement to others.

It is important to use truths from the Bible – the ones that tell you how God sees you as precious, loved and having a purpose and a hope and a future. God is a loving father who only wants our good.

Sadly the Bible can be used to portray God as other than loving, but that is due to a wrong handling of it. The Old Testament, I believe, often portrays God in the only way they could understand at the time. It took for Jesus to come to show us what God is really like.

There are numerous helpful, positive scriptures in the Bible that help raise our self-esteem and tell us that God truly loves and values us and that we have great worth.

In psalm 139, it says we are "fearfully and wonderfully made". In Isaiah 43 v 4, God says "you are precious and honoured in my sight, and….. I love you."

Some more encouragement is found in the scriptures in the section further on.

Faith and meaning

I am a believer in Jesus and my faith is very important to me in facing the challenges of life. In fact, I would find life very difficult, if not impossible, without knowing there was a higher purpose and deeper meaning to it than appears on the surface, and importantly knowing there is a God who is love.

Whatever your beliefs are or where you find meaning in life, it is important that they are helping you. People need meaning and to live for something outside themselves, whether it is bringing up a family or pursuing a career or serving a worthy cause. We need to find meaning and importance in what we are doing. We need to find enjoyment in that. We also need to find connection with people and be part of a community. For myself, being part of a local church community helps meet that need.

"It is not good for man to be alone."

You don't have to do something outstanding or newsworthy or become famous or rich for your life to be worthwhile. If that were the case, 99% of the population would find no fulfilment. Whilst the world celebrates achievement or being materially rich, some of the happiest and most content people are those who have found the way of using their gifts and talents to help others. Someone who is happy to do a menial job to the best of their ability can be happier than a millionaire.

Quoting Desiderata again:

"Enjoy your achievements as well as your plans. Keep interested in your own career, however, humble; it is a real possession in the changing fortunes of time."

Spiritual input

Whether you call yourself a Christian, (or a Muslim, Hindu, etc) or not, God loves you. People are often put off by religion or religious sounding words, but God is not religious. He is like the best in people because they are created in his image. Jesus came to show what God is really like and show the world a new way to live. He died because people, driven by pride, religion and politics, could not cope with him and the threat to their lifestyle that he posed. In dying, he took "the sin of the world" upon himself. He rose from the dead because death could not hold him. He showed us that we do not need to fear death because he overcame it. He sent his spirit to empower us to overcome the challenges we face and have the possibility of living life on a higher plane.

Encouragement from the Bible

There is power in reading scriptures such as those below and taking them to yourself. God is the Creator & Father of all humanity who cares about you and wants to speak into your life. Repeating these verses out loud and personalising them is helpful.

Scriptures are taken from the NIV version of the Bible.

The light shines in the darkness and the darkness has not overcome it.

John 1 v 5

You, Lord, keep my lamp burning; my God turns my darkness into light.

Psalm 18 v 28

Have no anxiety about anything, but in everything, with prayer and thanksgiving, let your requests be made known to God and the peace of God which passes all understanding, will guard your hearts and your minds in Christ Jesus.

Philippians 4 v 6-7

There is no fear in love but perfect love casts out fear.

1 John 4 v 18

You will keep in perfect peace those whose minds are steadfast, because they trust in you.

Isaiah 26.v 3

God is our refuge and strength, an ever-present help in trouble.

Therefore we will not fear, though the earth give way and the mountains fall into the heart of the sea, though its waters roar and foam and the mountains quake with their surging. There is a river whose streams make glad the city of God, the holy place where the Most High dwells. God is within her, she will not fall; God will help her at break of day.

Psalm 46 v 1-5

The Lord is compassionate and gracious, slow to anger, abounding in love.

And

As a father has compassion on his children, so the Lord has compassion on those who fear him; for he knows how we are formed, he remembers that we are dust.

Psalm 103

In fact, the whole of Psalm 103 is encouraging.

Whoever dwells in the shelter of the Most High will rest in the shadow of the Almighty. I will say of the Lord, "He is my refuge and my fortress, my God, in whom I trust."

Psalm 91v1-2

All of Psalm 91 is a wonderful protection Psalm.

Though the mountains be shaken and the hills be removed, yet my unfailing love for you will not be shaken nor my covenant of peace be removed, says the Lord, who has compassion on you.

Isaiah 54v10

Not just in our own strength

Yes we have to use our strength to get through depression. We can't just sit there and wait for it to pass, although perhaps that's all we can do at that moment.

But we need help. I think we need God's help. And that can come in many ways. Bear with me, if you don't believe this.

To be fair, we tend to make a bit of a mess of things when we go ahead and do things ourselves, according to our own desires and understanding, as wonderful and creative as we are. You only have to look around you to see that – whether it's the climate crisis and how we treat the planet or the wars and unrest around the world and how we treat one another. The way of self-interest and independence does not ultimately work. When we hit a personal crisis, we realise our own attempts to get ourselves out of the mess are often not quite enough. That's my experience anyway. I know I need God's help, the help of a kind, benevolent being who knows my frailties.

In depression we can feel very weak and helpless. Hopeless. Perhaps it's at these times we recognise our need for outside help the most and cry out to God.

As David says numerous times in the biblical psalms – God, help! Many of the psalms are psalms of lament.

> *"Answer me when I call to you, my righteous God. Give me relief from my distress; have mercy on me and hear my prayer."*
>
> *Psalm 4 v 1*

In psalm 6, David feels his suffering is from God and pleads with God:

> *"Lord, do not rebuke me in your anger or discipline me in your wrath. Have mercy on me, Lord, for I am faint, heal me, Lord, for my bones are in agony, my soul is in deep anguish, how long, Lord, how long?"*
>
> *Psalm 6 v 1-3*

I don't believe that God inflicts suffering on us as he is good and love, and nothing bad comes from him. The psalmist is expressing what he feels like – if God is in control, why doesn't he DO SOMETHING about my suffering? This is more a wrong understanding of God on mankind's part. He is not a master puppeteer who controls everything. God has given us choice, and when he gave mankind choice, he relinquished control.

I believe that our suffering can be a result of a complex variety of things – our experiences in this world, our make-up, our failings, others' actions or failure to act, how we react to life. You get the picture. Nothing to do with God. I do, however, believe that God will use suffering to make us more whole, if we allow it. It is counter intuitive that something painful and "bad" can be used to work for good but that is what God can do.

David, then, after pleading with God, declares that God is his refuge:

"Keep me safe, my God, for in you I take refuge."

Psalm 16 v 1.

For all his questioning of God, he knows God is where he can go for safety, refuge and help.

In times of distress, I have often gone to the psalms to find comfort and help. I have experienced receiving supernatural strength and peace from reading them, because as we mix our faith or trust or belief (whichever word works for you) with the words, there is power in them to heal us and impart good to us.

For example, when I read the 23rd psalm, it says:

"Even though I walk through the darkest valley, I will fear no evil, for you are with me." I am assured, in reading this, that in walking through the dark valley of depression, God is with me. It is an act of faith to believe that and claim it for yourself. Faith isn't just something relating to religious belief, we all exercise faith every day, whether we realise it or not, and it is essential for life. We all put our faith in people, our relationships, things, our work, and trust in things we can't see such as electricity.

Psalm 23 goes on to say, "You anoint my head with oil; my cup overflows." Oil speaks to me of healing. It's personalising the scriptures. There will be other ones that "speak" to you personally.

I have found that speaking the words out loud really helps and makes them more real. Doing this repeatedly can be likened to taking medicine and again the scripture does say this about itself.

See psalm 107 v 20 – "He (God) sent out his word and healed them" and Jesus said to his disciples in John 6 "The words I have spoken to you – they are full of the Spirit and life."

As a believer in Jesus, I am aware there is such a thing as a spiritual fight we are to engage in. As Christians, we believe Jesus has overcome the enemy, our role is to stand in that victory.

The speaker and author Joyce Meyer addresses this in her book "The Battlefield of the mind" and many people, whether they believe in God or not, recognise evil in the world. As the battlefield is in the mind, how we think is very important.

In Romans 12 v 2, the apostle Paul instructs believers to "be transformed by the renewing of your mind." That's because our minds naturally tend to negativity and defeatism many times. This is especially true when we are going through depression, but even if we are not, it is important to be aware of what we are allowing in our minds.

"Finally, brothers and sisters, whatever is true, whatever is noble, whatever is right, whatever is pure, whatever is lovely, whatever is admirable – if anything is excellent or praiseworthy – think about such things."

Phil 4 v.8

Thankfulness

I have found that thankfulness is a great habit to cultivate. It focusses our minds on what is positive rather than the negative. It makes us realise what we have. It's also good for others if we remember to thank them.

Perhaps that's why it's good to thank God and give him praise and worship. It chases away darkness and lifts our spirits. That's probably why God enjoys our praise and worship as he knows it benefits us. The bible says that God "inhabits the praises of his people".

Being thankful also strengthens our faith in God when we remember all he has done.

No matter how down we feel and how bad our circumstances are, there is always something we can be thankful for. When we are down, it's really hard to accept that but even if we can thank God for the breath we breathe, it will help us to start thinking of what we have.

Prayer

Prayer is also an important spiritual discipline and in my experience, a great help, especially if you are praying with someone else who likes to pray. It's good to pray on my own, but I can often go round in circles and get stuck, praying the same thing over and over. When I'm praying with someone else, it can flow more naturally and you can spark off each other.

We are all spirit, soul and body as human beings and the spiritual side has a very important part to play.

Without God's help I couldn't overcome depression. Thankfully he is an ever-present help in trouble. How often we underestimate that fact.

It can also be a help to ask for others to pray with or for us.

Hope

Knowing God and how he sees me and knowing there is an overall purpose and plan in life, gives me hope. Hope is essential in life and especially to overcome depression. I have to hope that I will get through this and that life can be better.

The scriptures describe hope as an anchor for the soul. An anchor stops you going adrift.

A Testimony

In this, my latest period of depression, I have at times felt desperation, as if I was sinking and unable to be rescued. I have had unpleasant feelings in my head and horrible thoughts. I went to our church meeting feeling unbalanced and vulnerable. After joining in with the worship, listening to an enlightening talk, I felt better. Then I took an older friend home and, as is our custom, we had a cuppa. I suggested we have a prayer time as we both like to pray. After this time, praying for others, as well as each other, I felt different. A shift had taken place.

Whether it was the lady's prayers for me or the fact I was praying for others, or being in agreement with this prayer partner, or all three, I don't know. All I know is I felt significantly better and for that I was grateful. I felt I'd been given a leg up. I know this isn't the end of it, I will still need to keep persevering.

I've noticed this happening before in my life – sometimes I seem to be struggling for what seems like ages, and then something changes. I think this shows the importance of perseverance and just keeping on. Then other times the cloud is there and I just can't seem to rise above it. At these times I need to trust God even more.

Just keep doing what you can. There IS hope, seriously. I don't know when your "shift" will come or how. Do you believe in God? He will help you. He will help you even if you don't believe in him, because he loves you.

Getting out of the vicious circle

We can get into self-defeating circles with depression. Our thoughts, feelings and behaviour can get into a vicious circle: -

Thoughts → Feelings-→ behaviour

Then our behaviour feeds into our thoughts, becoming a circle.

To break out of them we need to break the circle – Sometimes just doing something, will help us e.g. a household task or going for a walk. That's changing our behaviour. Or say or shout "stop" to the thoughts or switch to thinking something else, maybe by reading some of the scriptures I've listed or putting on some music. Music affects our emotions so this is a way of feeding a positive feeling into the circle.

A friend of mine, who had been in a long-term depression, had a breakthrough when she was looking after her son's dogs whilst he was on holiday. The routine of taking the dogs out for a walk and also digging up the dandelions in her son's lawn, helped break her to start to come out of depression. I suggest that these activities were enjoyable, grounding and helping someone else, and that all such activities like this can help us.

For myself, writing this book is helping me – using my skills of writing and typing and feeling I may be helping someone else ultimately – if it ever gets published!

I also enjoy ironing, knitting and pottering in the garden when the weather's better.

Things will get better

Believe this.

I believe that things can and will get better for you.

It will probably be a case of 2 steps forward and one step back (or in my case 2 or 3 steps back at times). So long as you are making some progress, sometimes, that's good. It can be a slow climb. It can be a slog.

And when you feel you're not getting anywhere or slump back into hopelessness and feel like giving up, be kind to yourself, have a rest, pick yourself up and carry on.

It's a long-distance trek, not a sprint.

Encourage yourself. Tell yourself you're doing okay; you'll get there in the end.

Our bodies and minds want to be healthy and I believe we have an in-built instinct to work towards health. The physical body has an inborn mechanism to heal itself and immediately, if damaged, goes into repair mode. I believe this is true of the mind also, but in depression, needs our help. It needs sleep, healthy food and exercise. As I mentioned previously, whilst we sleep, our spinal cord produces a fluid that helps detox our brains. That is amazing and I must admit that sometimes I have gone to sleep to escape my worries and awoken feeling much better in the morning. However, it doesn't always happen that way!

We also need good friends and people we can talk to. We need to do "what our soul loves" and what is meaningful to us.

But often, as I've said before, we may need medication for a time and professional help and counselling.

The good that comes from depression

It is difficult to see what good can come from an experience so difficult and unpleasant, but it certainly can.

Previously I have said that sometimes we experience depression when life just isn't working for us. So, depression can be a wake-up call for us; a time to evaluate what is important to us and where we need to focus our attention and energies next. It forces us to take stock and is an opportunity to work out what led us to be depressed and what is missing in our lives. It's a time to make a fresh start and find new meaning. To recognise what we need and what is important to us.

Another thing that depression can give us is more empathy and compassion for other people. Perhaps it shows you that you need to take a different approach to yourself and treat yourself with more kindness.

A CPN (community psychiatric nurse) once said to me that depression made people nicer afterwards. That was certainly a nice thought at the time.

Sometimes it's these little thoughts and throw away lines that we hear, that can really help us latch on to hope.

Seasons

Life has seasons. We learn from nature that this is the case and I believe that our lives go through seasons too.

We're not happy all the time nor should we be. Every emotion has its place. Every emotion is telling us something and can be constructive. Sometimes people think anger is wrong. But it is good to be angry – it's showing us we feel strongly about some injustice or our boundaries have been breached. We just have to manage how we express our anger. It's not good to repress it either.

What helps

Anti-Depressants

These are obviously prescribed by your GP and are usually SSRI's. There are various ones such as fluoxetine (also known as Prozac); sertraline; citalopram; venlafaxine, to name a few. They all operate in a similar way in helping your brain retain more of the chemicals that help you feel better.

However, I would say that there are side effects and you may feel worse before you feel better. This can be a real challenge, but it's worth persevering, for at least a few weeks as the anti-depressants take 4-6 weeks to start being effective.

Cognitive Behavioural Therapy (CBT)

This can be prescribed by your GP. Usually, you have to be referred to the Mental Health service and they will then ascertain what kind of counselling you would benefit from.

CBT is seen as effective in treating depression. I think there are different approaches used. When I first had it, the counsellor mainly looked at the kind of thoughts I was thinking and I was encouraged to fill out worksheets logging, the situation, how I felt and the thoughts I had been thinking that led to me feeling down. The idea was then to re-assess and change the thought to something more positive.

Another time, the counsellor explained the different negative thought patterns we can have and encouraged me to see where I was falling into these patterns. She also talked about core beliefs.

This current time I am going through CBT therapy; the approach is quite different and more helpful to me. I have been encouraged to keep a record of how I am spending each day, on a weekly basis and logging how my mood is at the end of the day. Usually, the pattern has emerged that if I am spending time with other people, my mood is more positive than if I have been on my own all day.

The goal I have been given is to just spend time with other people. To not feel I had to achieve anything else, e.g. impress anyone or make friends with anyone, but just to be there with people. This is because it was partly the feeling of isolation that had led to my depression.

Creativity

Doing something creative, helps us. It focuses our minds on what we are creating and gets us out of our internal dialogue. It is also rewarding to make something and gives us a sense of achievement.

Being creative includes:

Cooking

Knitting

Singing

Writing

Painting

Making things

Colouring

Gardening

Decorating your home or making it look nice.

The list is endless. You don't have to be a poet, musician or artist to be creative. You can be creative in helping someone else e.g. thinking of something that will cheer them up if they are down.

Meditation

This is something I'm new at but am finding it a benefit. It's not something spooky or necessarily religious (although it is found all the major religions), but an age-old practice of calming the mind and connecting with the inner part of yourself.

The practice involves sitting or lying in a comfortable position and focussing on your breath and breathing. You can also use a word such as "peace" or "love" to repeat internally as you breath. When thoughts come into your mind, as they will, just return to concentrating on your breath or your word, when you realise you've started engaging with those thoughts. This isn't easy and you'll wonder if you're "doing it right" but it will become easier. To get real benefit from this, you need to practice meditation daily.

I've found it beneficial to know I am letting go of those negative or repetitive or unpleasant thoughts. Or they may simply be thoughts about what you need to do or about other people. Letting them go and returning to focussing on your breathing or word, is a relief and is "the practice".

For people who are very anxious and have very busy minds, it will be difficult, especially at first but if you persevere, you will reap the benefits.

This practice of meditation is also good for calming your nervous system, which may have become "de-regulated" through trauma of some description.

Exercise

This is known to be helpful when you are depressed. It boosts your serotonin levels and helps you get out of your mind – I mean that in the healthiest way!

There's a lot of emphasis, it seems to me, on exercising these days and that is good, but if you're like me, someone who has an allergy to gyms and who hated PE at school, it is not always that attractive a proposition. However, I do enjoy a walk in the countryside and that is equally beneficial. Dancing is another type of exercise and with that, you have the benefit of music too.

Even doing some stretches can help you feel better. There's something about using your body in this way.

Famous people who have struggled with depression

I was watching a 2022 biopic on the actress Leslie Caron called "The Reluctant Star" in which she reveals that she has struggled with periods of severe depression in her life. She starred in the film "Gigi" amongst others and more recently in "The Durrells". At the end of the biopic, at age 92 she says:

"I looked for joy – there were some dark moments in my life of course, but I kept trying to find the solution, the light at the end of the black hole. That's the aim, that's what you have to do is to try, keep trying, keep trying. And it's never too late. I'm having very good times now, I find life absolutely wonderful and I'm very grateful......"

Another woman who has openly talked about her struggles with depression is Denise Welch, a well- known actress who used to be in Coronation Street and who is regularly one of the panellists in the TV programme "Loose Women". On one program, she said that the depression suddenly left and she hasn't been troubled with it anymore.

Conclusion

So, what have I learned on my journey?

I have learned that depression, as awful as it is, will not last forever.

I have learned that I need help to get through it, whether that is medical, counselling or support from friends or usually all three.

I have learned I have to do things myself such as reach out for help, walk or exercise, not neglect to be with people, and be creative.

I have also learned that God is there to help me. In my desperate times, when I have cried out to him, he has shown me he has not forgotten me and I have felt helped.

And finally, I have learned that good can come from going through depression. We can become more understanding of ourselves and others. It can lead us to search for new meaning and we find new purpose in life.

As I write this, several months after starting this book, I came off the anti-depressants weeks later, due to the side effects and fell into another spell of depression. I tried a new (to me) anti-depressant which I am now taking in the lowest dose, and after persevering with the side effects (which took some trusting), I am now feeling much better and able to enjoy life again. I have decided to stay on these for at least 6 months.

Postscript

I did not stay on them longer than 5 weeks as I felt the side effects becoming difficult. I have now been off them a few weeks and am feeling a lot better. This shows you just have to do what's right for you at that time.

Books I've found helpful

"Climbing out of depression" by Sue Atkinson

"I'm not supposed to feel like this" by Chris Williams, Paul Richards and Ingrid Whitton

"Brighter Days" by Patrick Regan

"The Battlefield of the Mind" by Joyce Meyer

"Finding Jesus in the Storm" {The spiritual lives of Christians with mental health challenges} by John Swinton

"Finding your hidden treasure" by Benignus O'Rourke (this is a great introduction to the benefits of meditation or silent prayer)

About the author

Julie was born & grew up in Letchworth, Hertfordshire. She moved north to study "Interdisciplinary Human Studies" at Bradford University where she became a Christian.

Having worked in various jobs she trained to be a social worker aged 39 & subsequently worked in both Children's & Adult Services. Now retired, she helps run a welcome space at the church she is part of in Keighley.

Thanks to my dear friends for being there for me (you know who you are), especially Eileen, Angela, Sandra, Val, Maddie & Thmes.

Thanks to my brothers & their families for their love.

Thanks to Moz for organising the publishing etc. when you already do a hundred and one things!

Thanks to my church family for being a community to belong to & accepting me as I am.

Printed in Great Britain
by Amazon